Pebble Plus

Exploremos la galaxia/Exploring the Galaxy
La Tierra/Earth

por/by Thomas K. Adamson

Traducción/Translation: Martín Luis Guzmán Ferrer, Ph.D.
Editor Consultor/Consulting Editor: Dra. Gail Saunders-Smith

James Gerard, Consultant
Aerospace Education Specialist, NASA
Kennedy Space Center, Florida

Capstone press

Mankato, Minnesota

Pebble Plus is published by Capstone Press
151 Good Counsel Drive, P.O. Box 669, Mankato, Minnesota 56002
http://www.capstone-press.com

1 2 3 4 5 6 11 10 09 08 07 06

Library of Congress Cataloging-in-Publication Data
Adamson, Thomas K.
    [Earth. Spanish & English]
    La Tierra = Earth / by Thomas K. Adamson.
    p. cm.—(Pebble plus: Exploremos la galaxia = Exploring the galaxy)
    English and Spanish.
    Includes index.
    ISBN-13: 978-0-7368-5878-6 (hardcover)
    ISBN-10: 0-7368-5878-4 (hardcover)
    1. Earth—Juvenile literature. I. Title: Earth. II. Title.
QB631.4.A3318 2005
550—dc22   2005019040

Summary: Simple text and photographs describe planet Earth.

Editorial Credits
Mari C. Schuh, editor; Kia Adams, designer; Alta Schaffer, photo researcher; Eida del Risco, Spanish copy editor; Jenny Marks, bilingual editor

Photo Credits
Bruce Coleman Inc./Phil Degginger, 16–17
Corbis Images, 19
Digital Vision, 5 (Venus)
Digital Wisdom, 13
Image Source, 20–21
NASA, 1, 4 (Pluto); JPL, 5 (Jupiter); JPL/Caltech, 5 (Uranus); NSSDC, 15
PhotoDisc Inc., cover, 4 (Neptune), 5 (Mars, Mercury, Earth, Sun, Saturn), 7 (both), 8–9; PhotoDisc Imaging, 11

Note: When Earth is viewed from space, Earth's north is not always oriented "up."

Note to Parents and Teachers

The Exploremos la galaxia/Exploring the Galaxy series supports national standards related to earth and space science. This book describes Earth in both English and Spanish. The photographs support early readers and language learners in understanding the text. Repetition of words and phrases helps early readers and language learners learn new words. This book also introduces early readers to subject-specific vocabulary words, which are defined in the Glossary section. Early readers may need assistance to read some words and to use the Table of Contents, Glossary, Internet Sites, and Index sections of the book.

Table of Contents

Tabla de contenidos

Earth

Earth is the only planet in the solar system where people and animals live. Earth and the other planets move around the Sun.

La Tierra

La Tierra es el único planeta del sistema solar donde la gente y los animales pueden vivir. La Tierra y los demás planetas se mueven alrededor del Sol.

4

The Solar System/El sistema solar

Earth/La Tierra

Sun/El Sol

It takes about 365 days
for Earth to move around
the Sun one time. Earth
moves around the Sun
once each year.

La Tierra tarda cerca de
365 días en darle una vuelta
al Sol. La Tierra se mueve
alrededor del Sol una vez
al año.

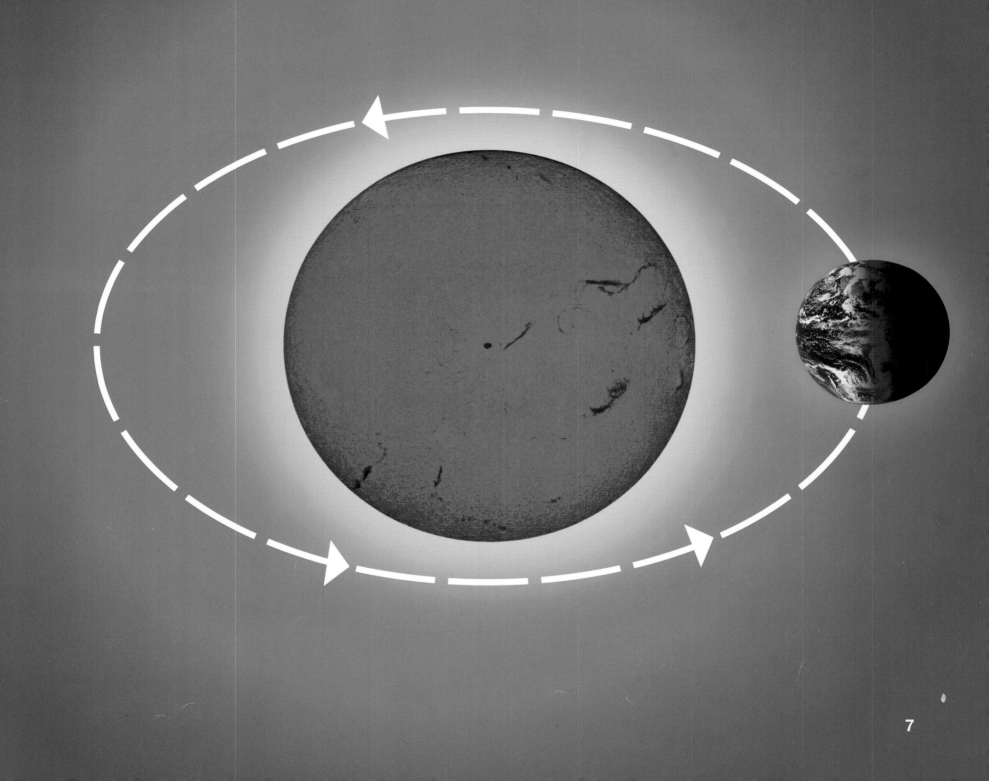

Air and Land

People and animals breathe the air on Earth. Life cannot survive without air.

Aire y tierra

La gente y los animales respiran el aire de la Tierra. La vida no puede existir sin el aire.

Earth is made of rock
and metal. The center of
Earth is hot molten metal.

La Tierra está formada de roca
y metal. El centro de la Tierra
es de metal fundido muy caliente.

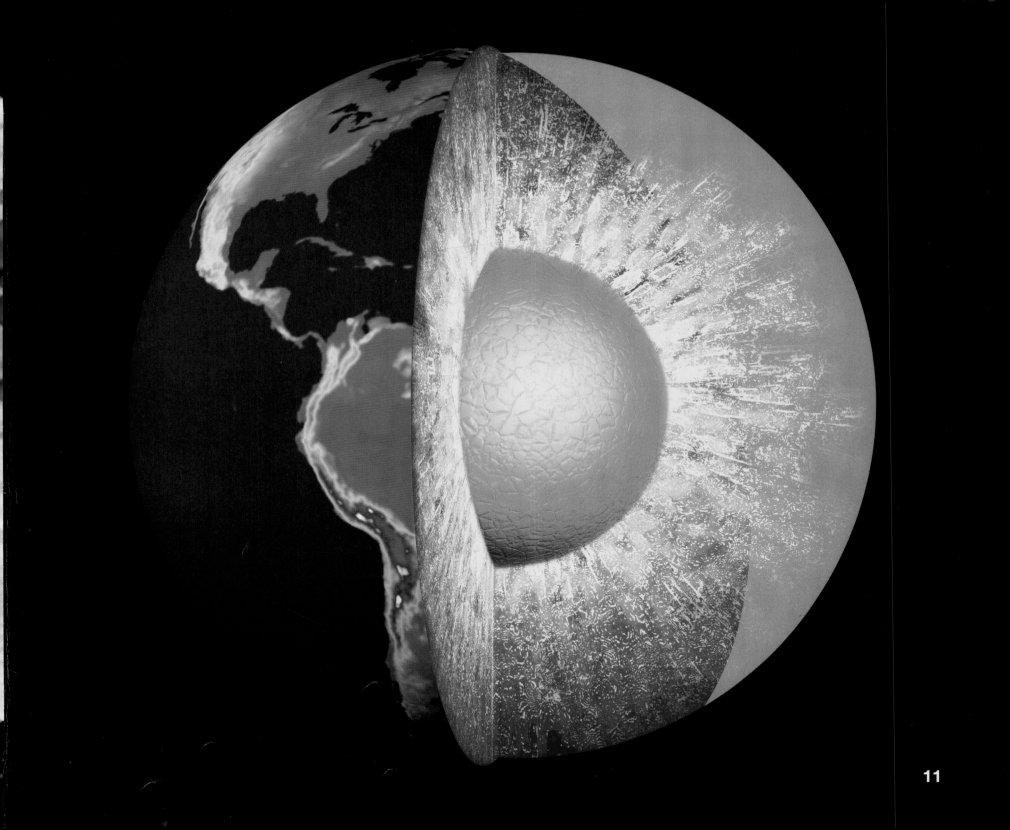

Water

Water covers most of
Earth's surface. People
and animals cannot
survive without water.

Agua

El agua cubre la mayor parte
de la superficie de la Tierra.
La gente y los animales no
pueden vivir sin agua.

13

Most of Earth's water is in
the oceans. The water makes
Earth look blue from space.

La mayor parte del agua de
la Tierra está en los océanos.
El agua hace que la Tierra
se vea azul desde el espacio.

Weather

Earth has many types
of weather. Different
places on Earth get
different kinds of weather.

Clima

La Tierra tiene muchos tipos
de clima. Los diferentes
lugares de la Tierra tienen
diferentes clases de clima.

People and Earth

Earth has one moon.

People can easily see

the Moon from Earth.

La gente y la Tierra

La Tierra sólo tiene una luna.

La gente puede ver la Luna

fácilmente desde la Tierra.

Earth gives people and
animals all they need to live.
Earth has air, food, water,
and the right temperature.

La Tierra les da a la gente
y a los animales todo lo que
necesitan para vivir. La Tierra
tiene aire, alimento, agua
y la temperatura correcta.

Glossary

molten—melted by heat

moon—an object that moves around a planet; Earth has one moon.

ocean—a large body of salt water; the five oceans of Earth are the Atlantic, Pacific, Arctic, Antarctic, and Indian Oceans.

planet—a large object that moves around the Sun; Earth is the third planet from the Sun; there are nine planets in the solar system.

Sun—the star that the planets move around; the Sun provides light and heat for the planets.

weather—the conditions outside; weather can be hot or cold, wet or dry, calm or windy, or clear or cloudy.

year—the period of time in which Earth makes one trip around the Sun; one year is about 365 days.

Glosario

año—el periodo de tiempo que tarda la Tierra en hacer un viaje alrededor del Sol; un año es cerca de 365 días.

clima—las condiciones en el exterior; el clima puede ser caluroso o frío, lluvioso o seco, tranquilo o con viento, despejado o nublado.

fundido—derretido por el calor

luna—un objeto que se mueve alrededor de un planeta; la Tierra tiene una luna.

océano—un cuerpo grande de agua salada; los cinco océanos de la Tierra son el Atlántico, el Pacífico, el Ártico, el Antártico y el Índico.

planeta—un objeto grande que se mueve alrededor del Sol; la Tierra es el tercer planeta a partir del Sol; hay nueve planetas en el sistema solar.

Sol—la estrella alrededor de la cual se mueven los planetas; el Sol les proporciona luz y calor a los planetas.

Internet Sites

Do you want to find out more about Earth and the solar system? Let FactHound, our fact-finding hound dog, do the research for you.

Here's how:

1) Visit **www.facthound.com**

2) Type in the **Book ID** number: **0736821112**

3) Click on **FETCH IT.**

FactHound will fetch Internet sites picked by our editors just for you!

Sitios de Internet

¿Quieres saber más sobre la Tierra y el sistema solar? Deja que FactHound, nuestro perro sabueso, haga la investigación por ti.

Así:

1) Ve a **www.facthound.com**

2) Teclea el número ID del libro: **0736821112**

3) Clic en **FETCH IT.**

¡Facthound buscará en los sitios de Internet que han seleccionado nuestros editores sólo para ti!